Around the World
COLORING
BOOK

ACKNOWLEDGEMENTS

Commissioned and project managed by Twist Publishing
Author: Claire Sipi
Design: Craig and Kait Eaton at Duck Egg Blue
Illustrator: Eva Byrne
Publishing Director: Piers Pickard
Publisher: Hanna Otero
Commissioning Editor: Rhoda Belleza
Print Production: Lisa Ford

Published in June 2019 by Lonely Planet Global Ltd

CRN: 554153
ISBN: 9781788681124

www.lonelyplanetkids.com

Printed in Malaysia
10 9 8 7 6 5 4 3 2 1

MIX
Paper from responsible sources
FSC™ C021741

Paper in this book is certified against the Forest Stewardship Council™ standards. FSC™ promotes environmentally responsible, socially beneficial and economically viable management of the world's forests.

STAY IN TOUCH
lonelyplanet.com/contact

Lonely Planet Offices AUSTRALIA The Malt Store, Level 3, 551 Swanston St, Carlton, Victoria 3053 T: 03 8379 8000
IRELAND Digital Depot, Roe Lane (off Thomas St), Digital Hub, Dublin 8, D08 TCV4
USA 124 Linden St, Oakland, CA 94607 T: 510 250 6400 5100
UK 240 Blackfriars Rd, London SE1 8NW T: 020 3771 5100

lonely planet kids

Around the World COLORING BOOK

Written by Claire Sipi

Illustrated by Eva Byrne

Contents

The map to your book!

Welcome to your worldwide festival tour! No matter where we live or what culture we come from, we all celebrate to mark important events and days. From colorful carnivals to delicate cherry blossoms, religious holy days to spectacular fireworks, magnificent feasts to ritual dances, get ready to color your way around the globe. Enjoy the party!

Don't forget to pack your colored pencils and pens for coloring along the way!

Europe

p30

East Asia

p54

Africa and the Middle East

p42

Australia and Southeast Asia

p66

Turn the page to start your journey.

North America

From themed carnival floats, street musicians, and tribal dances to flying balloons over the desert and historical celebrations, North America's festivals are as varied as its people.

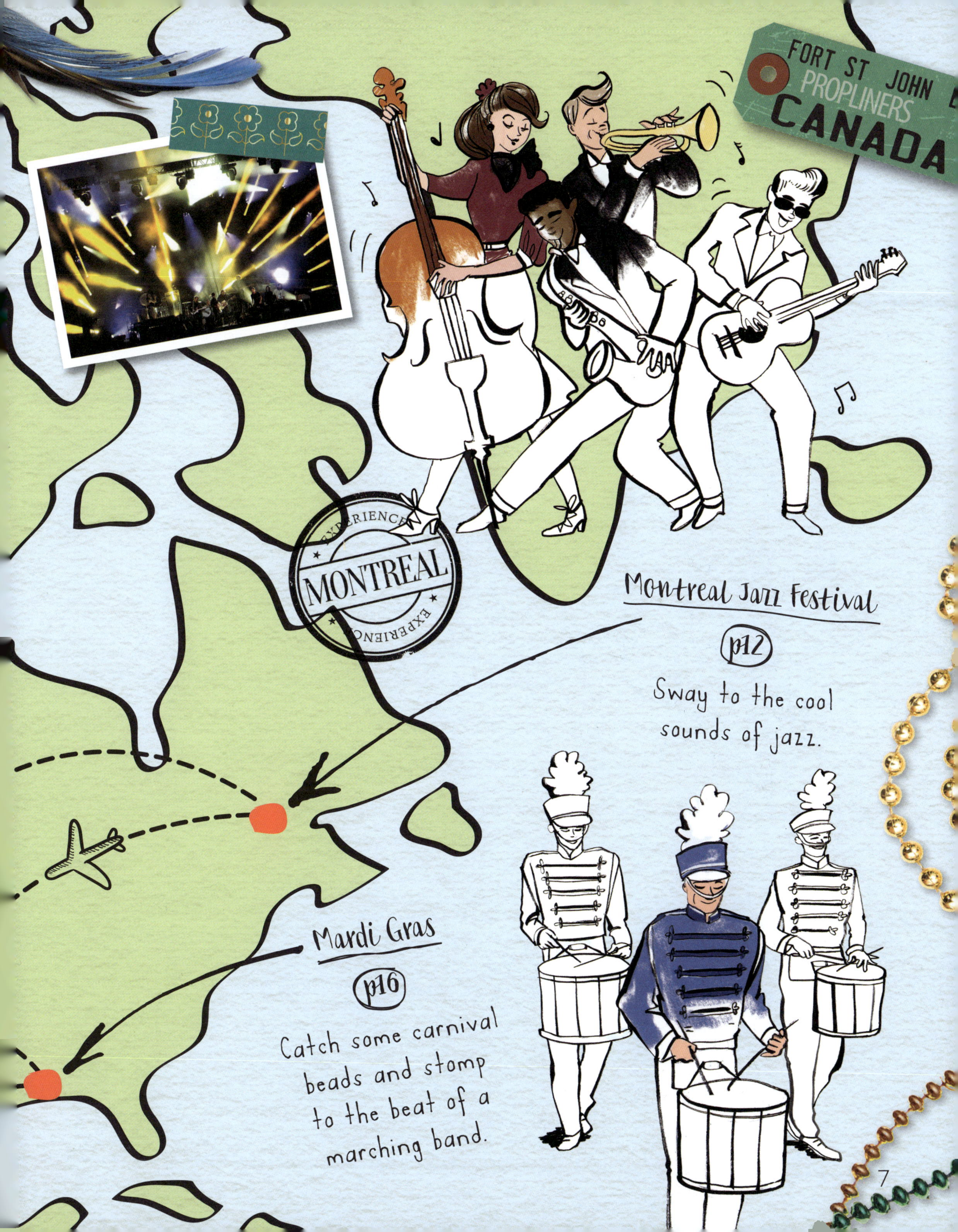
FORT ST JOHN
PROPLINERS
CANADA
EXPERIENCE
MONTREAL
EXPERIENCE
Montreal Jazz Festival
p12
Sway to the cool sounds of jazz.
Mardi Gras
p16
Catch some carnival beads and stomp to the beat of a marching band.

Independence Day

All across the USA on the Fourth of July, people celebrate the 1776 Declaration of Independence and the birth of the nation. There are huge street parties, parades, and fireworks.

Many people dress up in the red, white, and blue colors of the flag.

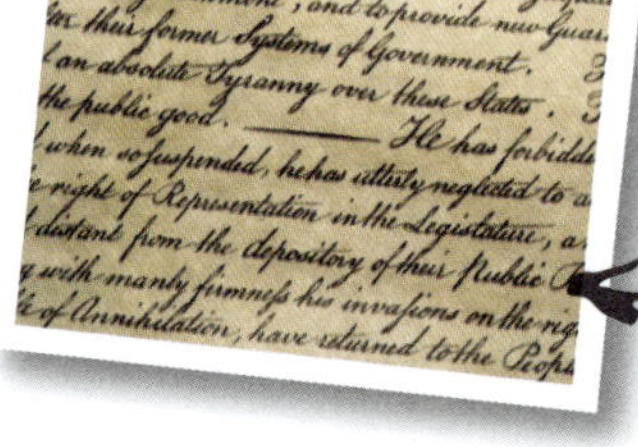

them shall seem most likely to effect their
accordingly all experience hath shewn, that
But when a long train of abuses and
such Government, and to provide new
their former Systems of Government.
an absolute Tyranny over these States.
the public good. —— He has
when so suspended, he has utterly neglected to
right of Representation in the Legislature,
distant from the depository of their Public
with manly firmness his invasions on the
of Annihilation, have returned to the

The Declaration of Independence declared the USA's independence from Great Britain.

Firework displays are a huge part of the holiday!

Parades can include music, dancing, and giant inflatables.

Stilt walkers dress as Uncle Sam, a character who represents the USA.

Powwow

For Native American and First Nations tribes, a powwow is a time to celebrate traditions and make friends. Different peoples gather to dance, parade, and take part in friendly competitions.

The United Tribes International Powwow in North Dakota is one of the largest powwows.

Many people wear traditional dress. This woman is wearing the clothes of the Oglala Lakota tribe.

In the jingle dance, metal cones sewn on to the dress make a jingling sound as the dancer moves.

The jingle dance is traditionally performed to help heal the sick.

Hoop dancers spin and twirl many hoops to make amazing shapes.

Montreal Jazz Festival

If you want to experience the cool funky sounds of jazz music, Montreal is the place to visit in the summer. Around 3,000 artists from more than 30 different countries perform in one of the largest jazz events in the world!

Need to know:

Jazz was invented by African-American musicians. It comes from a blend of African and Spanish music, mixed with the beats of a brass band.

Musicians often improvise (make up) tunes as they play.

The five emblems on Montreal's coat of arms represent the city's five founding peoples.

Albuquerque Balloon Fiesta

Up, up and away! The Albuquerque International Balloon Fiesta is the largest hot-air balloon event in the world. Pilots come from all over the world to show off their balloons and compete in balloon-flying competitions.

During the Dawn Patrol, pilots take off before sunrise. They fly until it is light enough to see a landing site.

USA

Need to know:

Weather conditions have to be just right. If it is too windy, the balloons can't be launched.

"Hoot-hoot"

At night, pilots turn on their burners to create a display of glowing inflated balloons.

Mardi Gras

The festival of Mardi Gras is party time in New Orleans! The streets are filled with parades of decorated floats. Crowds of people wear fancy dress, beads and masks, dance to jazz and marching bands, and eat delicious food.

A marching band plays their instruments while walking along!

Snare drum

USA

Traditionally, a carnival king threw fake gems into the crowds. Today, strings of coloured beads are thrown instead.

The King Cake is decorated like a jewelled crown. It honours the three kings who visited baby Jesus in the Christian religion.

Mardi Gras' official colours are green (faith), gold (power), and purple (justice).

The fleur-de-lis symbol of New Orleans was once used by French royalty. It celebrates the city's French heritage.

Day Of the Dead

Every November, Mexican families get together for two days of festivities to remember the dead. Skull-shaped sweets and ornaments are everywhere, people dress up as skeletons, and prayers are said to ask the dead to return for just one night.

Families decorate the graves of their relatives.

Sugar skulls

Hand-painted wooden skulls represent the souls of the dead.

Carnival float

Need to know:

The first day of the festival is dedicated to dead children and the second to dead adults.

People get dressed up in old-fashioned clothes and use black-and-white makeup to make their faces look like skulls.

Central and South America

Central and South American festivals embrace hope and change. They combine history, ritual, and honoring ancestors with a sense of energy and fun.

Feria de Las Flores

p22

A fragrant festival of flowers.

Candelaria

p26

Parade, dance, pray, and feast!

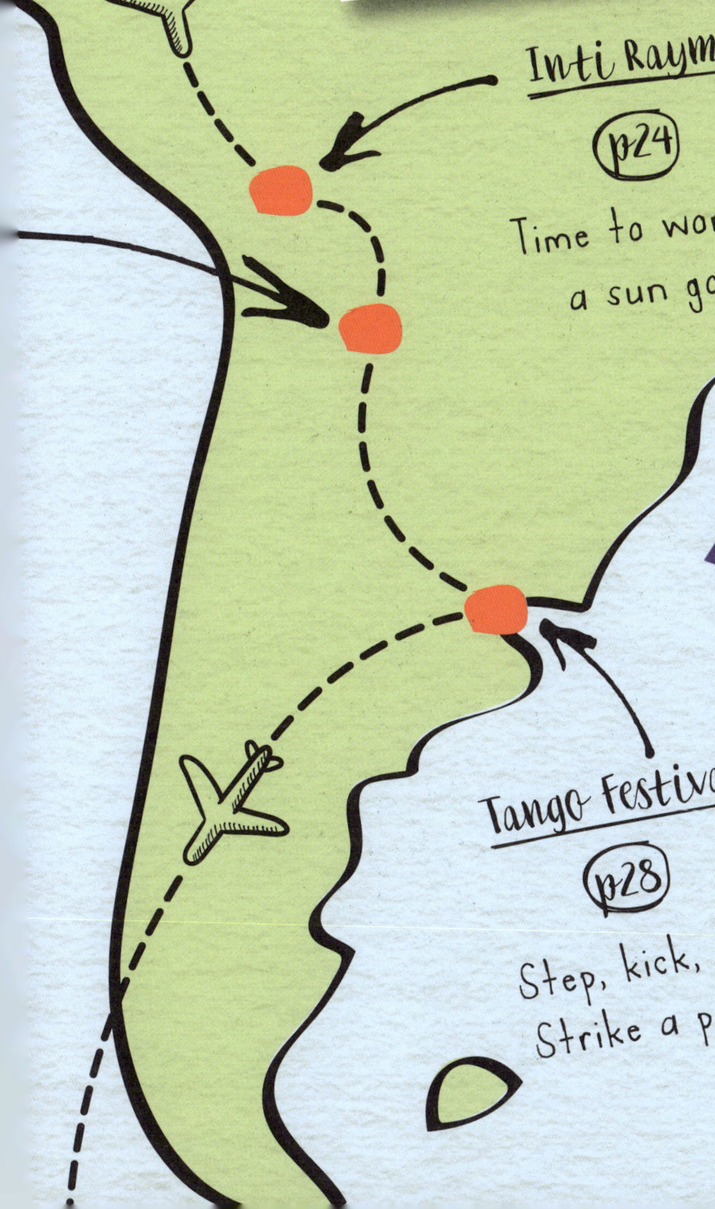
Inti Raymi
p24
Time to worship a sun god.
Tango Festival
p28
Step, kick, dip! Strike a pose!

Feria de las Flores

Colombia's Feria de las Flores celebrates Colombia's flower growers. In the Desfile de Silleteros (flower-growers parade), huge hand-crafted flower displays are carried through the streets.

Need to know:

Colombia's climate is perfect for growing flowers, and Colombian flowers are sold all over the world.

Giant garlands featuring flowers such as carnations, roses, and sunflowers are created.

The silleteros carry the garlands on their backs. The garlands can weigh up to 150 pounds!

Wooden frame

Silletero means "flower grower."

Amazing flower sculptures are created as well as garlands.

Inti Raymi

The Incas worshipped the sun god, Inti. Inti Raymi is a reenactment of their festival honoring him. Thousands of people watch an elaborate procession from the town of Cuzco to the Inca ruins of Sacsayhuamán.

In the procession, actors play the roles of ancient Incas.

Staff

Sacsayhuamán

The actor playing Sapa Inca (king of the Incas) dresses in a fabulously colored costume.

Try these colors.

PERU

The festival also celebrates Peruvian music and culture.

The sun god Inti is usually represented as a sun with a human face.

Need to know:

The Incas ruled one of the largest empires in the world in the 1400s and 1500s. Many people in Peru are descended from them.

Candelaria

Every February on the shores of Lake Titicaca, the sleepy fishing village of Copacabana comes alive for three days of partying. Dancing, music, feasting, and parades all celebrate Bolivia's patron saint, the Virgen de la Candelaria.

A statue of the Virgen de la Candelaria is carried through the streets.

Woolen hat with ear flaps

Woven poncho

Musicians parade playing wooden pipes and drums.

In Christianity a saint is someone who is recognized as being particularly close to God.

Lake Titicaca

Tango Festival

Step onto the dance floor—it's tango time! Every August the Argentine capital Buenos Aires goes wild for the world's largest tango event. Dance parties (milongas), competitions, tango orchestras, and films all celebrate the country's most famous dance.

The festival finishes with the Tango World Cup, where over 500 couples compete to reach the finals at Luna Park.

In tango, two people always dance as a pair.

ARGENTINA

Need to know:

Tango was invented at the end of the 1800s in the poor port area of Buenos Aires. It wasn't long before tango fever hit Europe and then the rest of the world!

Join one of the many free festival dance classes to learn the moves.

Europe

Experience culture, history, costumes, masks, concerts, huge street parties, festive treats . . . and discover a city where it doesn't get dark in the summer!

Did you know that Russia's so big it's in two continents: Asia AND Europe?

St Patrick's Day

p32

Saints and street parties!

Weihnachten

p36

Merry Christmas from Germany!

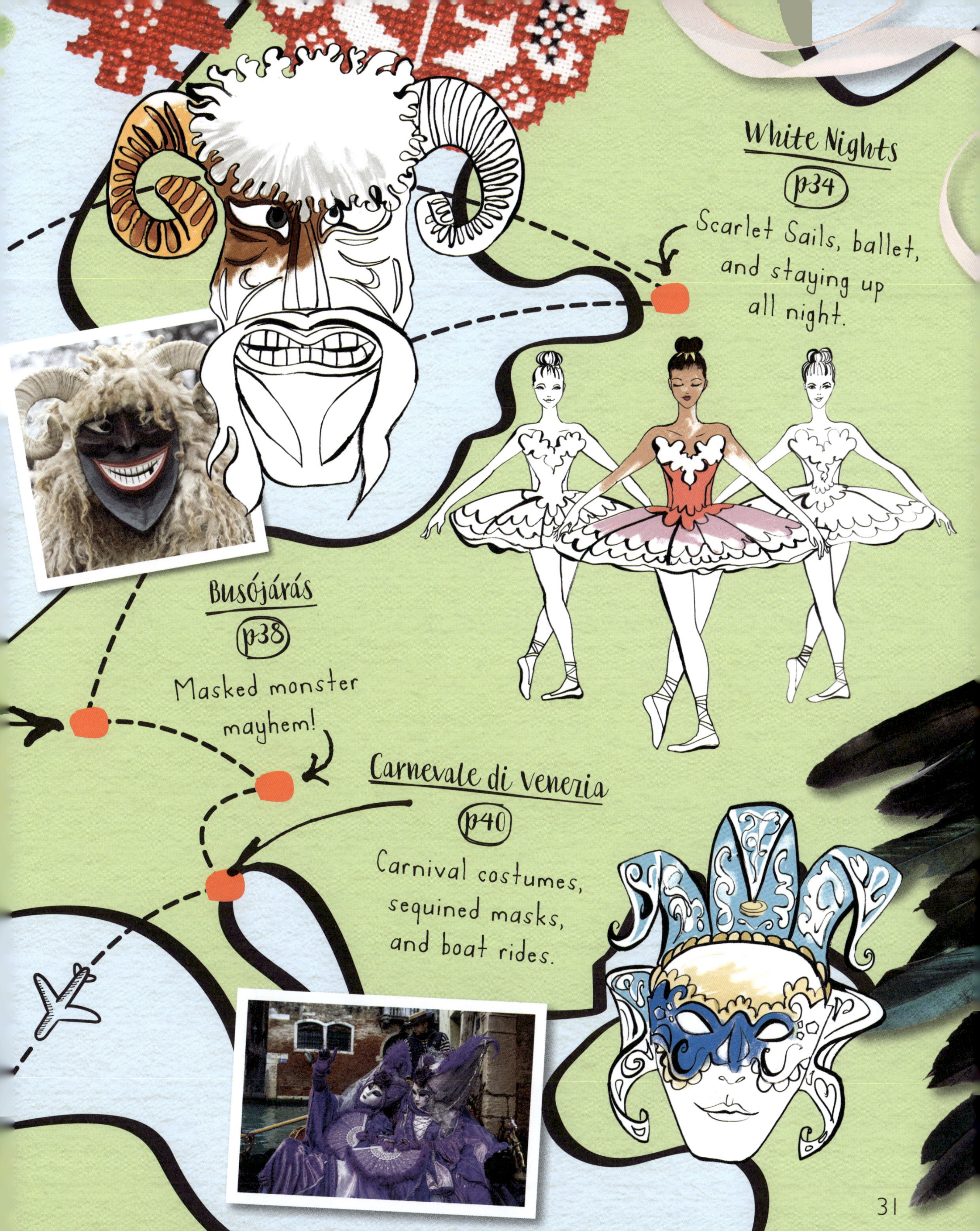
White Nights
p34
Scarlet Sails, ballet, and staying up all night.
Busójárás
p38
Masked monster mayhem!
Carnevale di Venezia
p40
Carnival costumes, sequined masks, and boat rides.

St Patrick's Day

Go to any city in Ireland on St Patrick's Day and you'll find yourself at one of the world's biggest parties! Hundreds of thousands of people gather on streets across Ireland to dance, feast, and parade in celebration of the country's patron saint, St Patrick.

Need to know:

St Patrick's Day is held every year on March 17, the anniversary of the death of St Patrick.

Dance costumes are embroidered with swirling Celtic designs.

Traditional Irish dancing involves lots of quick, precise foot movements.

People dress in green and play Irish folk songs on wind and brass instruments.

Green is the color of the shamrock plant, a symbol of St Patrick and of Ireland.

Stained glass window showing St Patrick. One legend says he got rid of all the snakes in Ireland by chasing them into the sea!

White Nights

Did you know that at midsummer in St Petersburg, it never gets dark? The Russian city celebrates these "White Nights" (Beliye Nochi) with special events, late-night concerts, and ballets.

In the Scarlet Sails event, a giant crimson sailing ship travels up the River Neva towards the Winter Palace.

Spectacular fireworks accompany the ship's journey.

The famous Mariinsky Theatre hosts many events.

Need to know:

St Petersburg is one of the world's northernmost cities. Places in the far north or south of the globe have extra-long days in the summer—and extra-long nights in the winter!

Because the sun only dips just below the horizon, twilight lasts all night long.

Russian ballet is world famous, and ballet shows are always part of the White Nights festival.

Weihnachten

Frohe Weihnachten! (Merry Christmas!) Visit Germany during the Christmas holiday season and you'll be able to taste delicious festive treats, listen to choirs and bands, and buy gifts at one of the many bustling Christmas markets.

The evergreen Christmas tree is a symbol of everlasting life.

People often decorate their trees with angels and stars.

GERMANY

The atmosphere at a Christmas market is magical, with choirs singing carols and twinkling lights everywhere.

Gingerbread biscuits with icing on top, called Lebkuchen, are a traditional treat. Yum!

In Germany, St Nicholas (Sankt Nikolaus) visits children on December 6 and leaves small gifts in their shoes.

Busójárás

Every winter, men dressed as horned characters called Busós take to the streets of the town of Mohács in Hungary. Their job is to see winter off with lots of noise and mischief-making!

The Busós parade through the town, teasing passersby and shaking noisemakers to create a racket!

Each Busó mask is unique.

On the final evening of the festival, the Busós burn a coffin to signify the death of winter.

Need to know:

The festival dates back to a time when the villagers of Mohács dressed up in fearsome masks to scare away an attacking Turkish army.

Carnevale di Venezia

Go to Venezia (Venice) during the annual Carnevale and you'll find the whole city wearing masks and fancy-dress costumes! For about two weeks every year, everyone gets to pretend to be someone else—and join in a huge party.

A competition for the best mask is held.

Boats float along the winding canals carrying elaborately dressed passengers.

Need to know:

Carnevale happens just before Lent, a Christian festival. Traditionally it's the last time to eat rich foods such as sweets before giving them up for 40 days!

The long-nosed Medico della Peste (Plague Doctor) mask is one of the best-known types of masks.

Beads, feathers, gems, and gold and silver are used to decorate the masks.

Africa and the Middle East

A month of fasting, spiritual mask dances, mass baptisms, and a beauty pageant like no other! The festivals in Africa and the Middle East are as varied as the extraordinary cultures of the region.

Masks Festival

p44

Communicate with spirits from the natural world.

Gerewol

p46

A beauty pageant to impress future brides!

Ramadan

p48

Fasting and feasts.

Hanukkah

p50

A festival of lights and the story of a miracle.

Timkat

p52

Processions and mass baptisms.

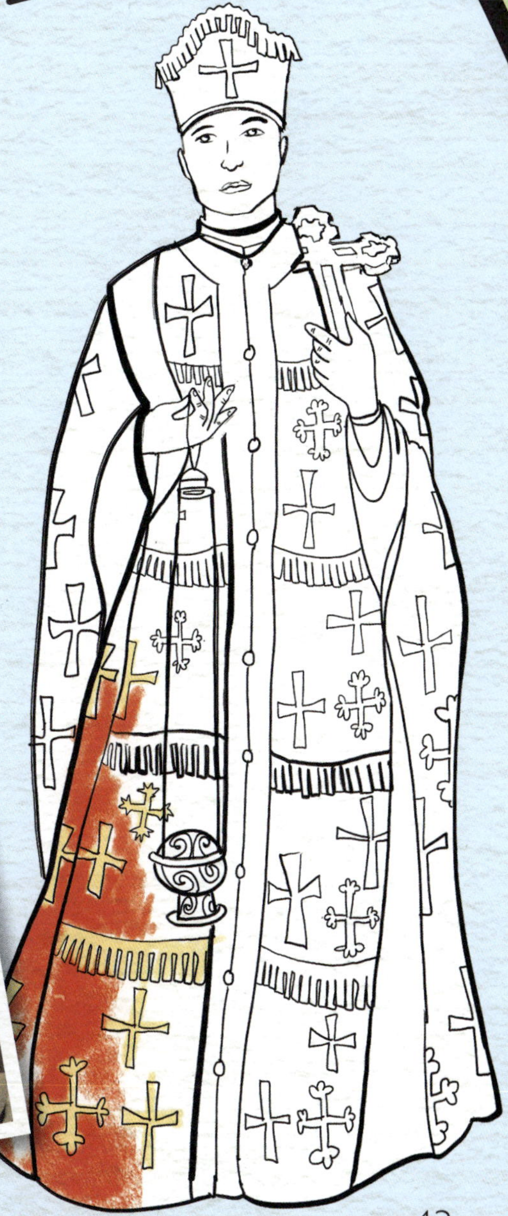

Masks Festival

Dancers in carved and tasseled masks spin and stomp to the pulse of drums and traditional African instruments. Welcome to FESTIMA—the International Festival of Masks and Arts in Burkina Faso.

People believe that the fast moves of the dances transform the mask-wearer into a spirit.

The hand-crafted masks symbolize the worship of ancestors and spirits from the natural world.

Geometric shapes are carved in wood.

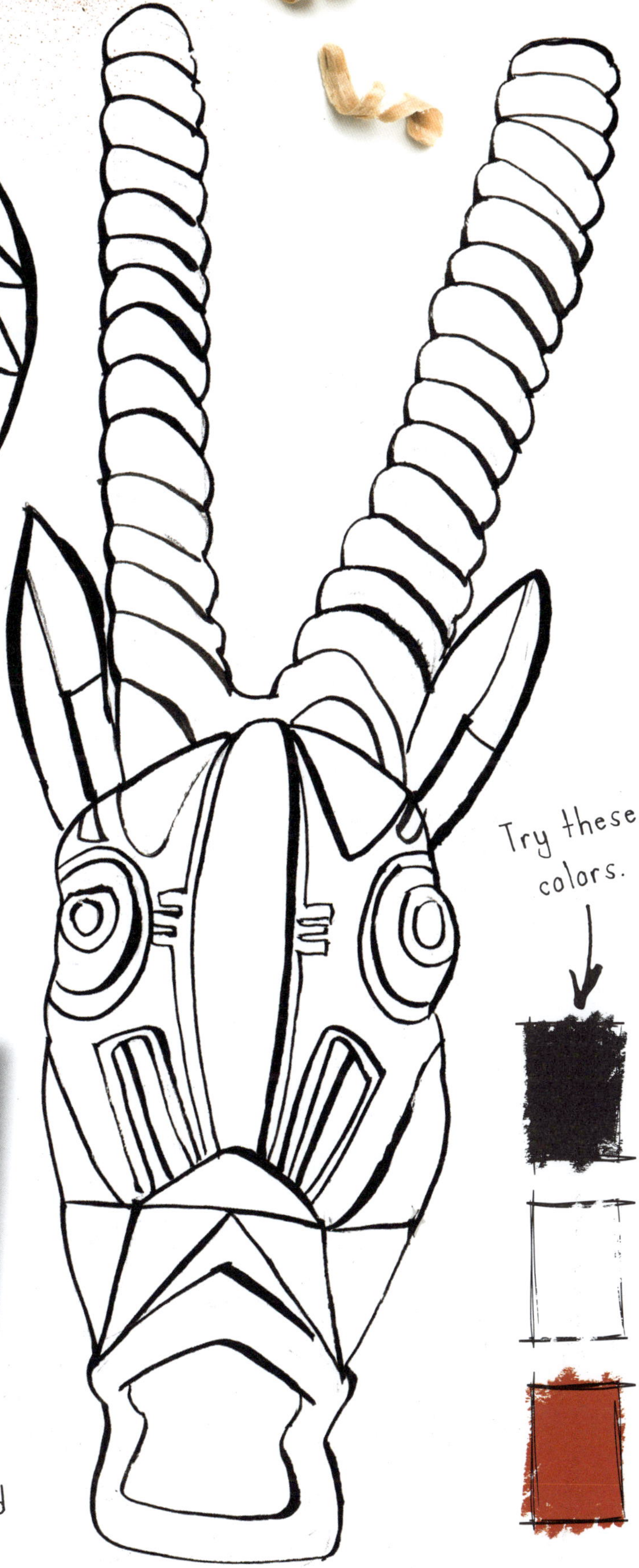

Try these colors.

There are masks not just from Burkina Faso but from countries all over West Africa!

Some masks are designed to look like animals or birds. Others are fish-shaped or covered in leaves like a tree.

Gerewol

In Niger, the Wodaabe people gather every year to hold Gerewol beauty pageants. Young men who want to get married dress up elaborately and dance for hours to impress possible brides.

NIGER

Need to know:

Gerewols take place on the southern edge of the Sahara Desert, at the end of the rainy season.

The men paint their faces.

The competition is fierce. Contestants grin widely and roll their eyes to show their bright eyes and white teeth.

Ramadan

Each year during the month of Ramadan, Muslims in Turkey and around the world avoid all food and drink between sunrise and sunset. The end of Ramadan is celebrated with the three-day festival of Eid al-Fitr (Arabic for "breaking of the fast").

At Eid, Muslims eat special meals and sweet treats, exchange gifts, and give food to the poor.

During Ramadan, mosques are extra busy with people saying special prayers.

Sultan Ahmed mosque, Istanbul

Need to know:

A mosque is a Muslim place of worship. The famous Sultan Ahmed mosque in Istanbul is also known as the Blue Mosque.

Inside the Sultan Ahmed mosque are amazingly intricate tiles and stained glass, all with a blue theme!

Hanukkah

Hanukkah is the eight-day Jewish festival of lights. It celebrates the miracle of the oil lamp. Jews in Israel and around the world believe that after the Temple of Jerusalem was destroyed, God kept the Temple lamp lit for eight days, even though there was only enough oil for one day.

The ninth candle (called the shamash) is used to light the other eight.

Each day of the festival, families light one more candle on a candlestick called a menorah.

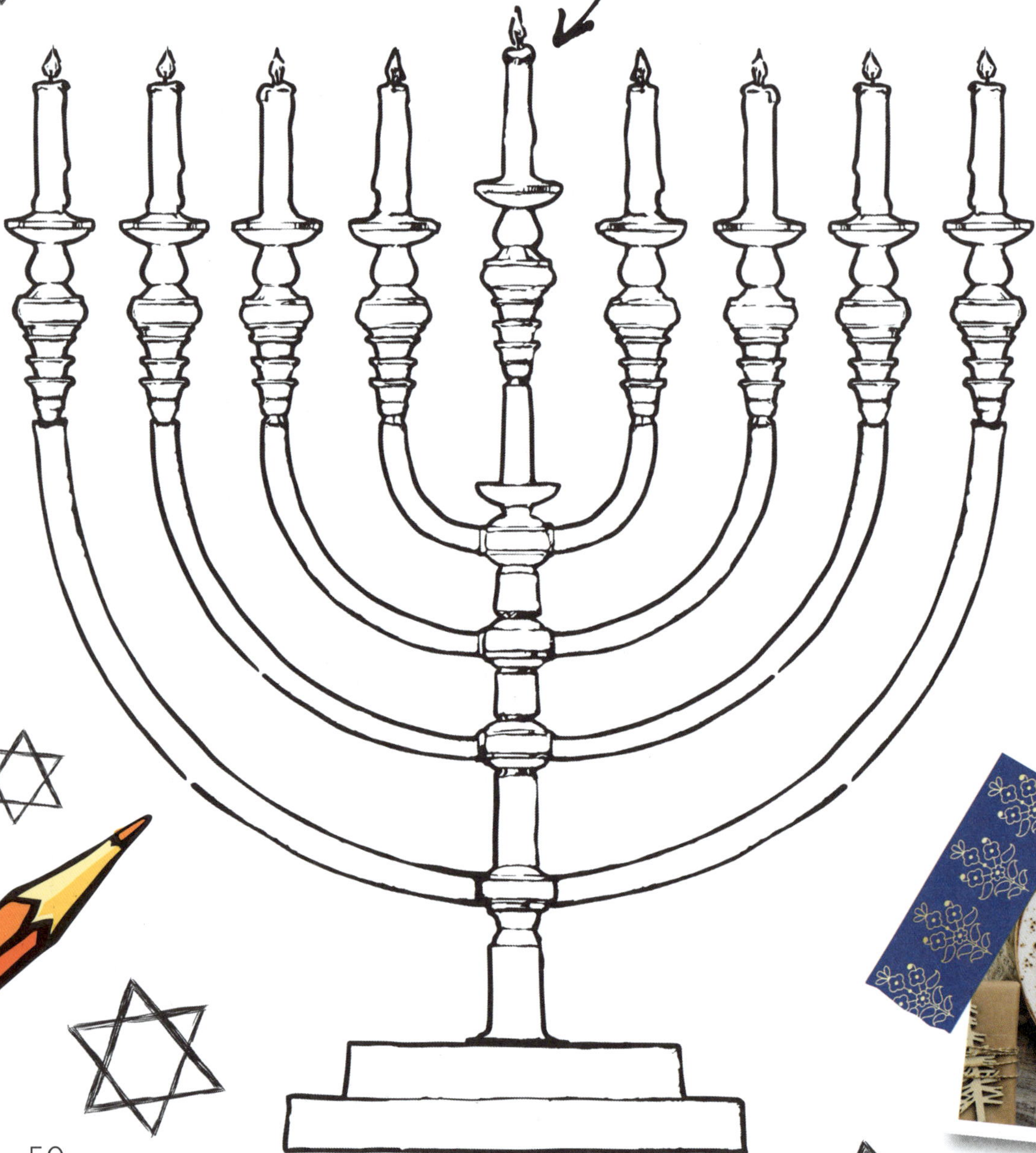

People eat food fried in oil, such as latkes (potato pancakes), to remember the miracle.

The Hebrew letters on a dreidel top are the first letters of the phrase "A great miracle happened there."

People play a game called dreidel. Spin a top and try to win as many counters (or sweets) as possible!

Timkat

Timkat means "baptism" in Amharic (an Ethiopian language). In the Timkat festival Ethiopian Christians celebrate Jesus' baptism in the River Jordan with processions, dancing, music, feasting, and a mass baptism.

Priests bless the waters of a public bath so that everyone who wants to can be baptized!

Need to know:

Baptism is a Christian ceremony where water is sprinkled on to a person to symbolize that they have joined the Christian Church.

The priests' elaborate robes are specially blessed and only worn when worshipping.

Try these colors.

ETHIOPIA

Accompanied by drum beats, the priests dance and sing as they lead the worshippers in procession.

Try these colors.

The priests carry huge, beautifully decorated umbrellas.

East Asia

Many Asian festivals welcome in the new year or celebrate the start of spring. There are colorful lanterns, spectacular blossoms, and skillful sporting events. They celebrate hope and renewal, and the triumph of good over evil.

Diwali

p56

The triumph of light over darkness.

Naadam

p60

Let the games begin!

Chinese New Year

p58

"Gong xi fa cai!" Wishing you great happiness and prosperity.

Pingxi Lantern Festival

p62

Time to send out wishes for a new year.

Yeouido Cherry Blossom Festival

p64

Spring is in the air!

Diwali

Diwali is a festival of lights, traditionally celebrated by Hindus, Jains, Sikhs and some Buddhists. Also known as Deepavali, it symbolizes new beginnings, the triumph of light over darkness, and good over evil.

People light small oil lamps called diyas and let off fireworks.

Rangoli patterns are created on floors using rice, spices, sand, and petals.

Need to know:

Lakshmi (Hindu goddess of prosperity and good fortune) and Ganesh (Hindu god of wisdom) are often worshipped at Diwali.

Everyone snacks on specially made sweet treats.

Try these colors.

Chinese New Year

Chinese New Year festivities are loud and colorful! There is feasting, dancing, music, fireworks, and spectacular dragon and lion dances. People celebrate to welcome good luck and health, wealth, and happiness into the coming year.

People dress in red (a lucky color in China) to scare evil spirits away.

Lion dance troupes visit shops and houses.

Inside the amazing lion costume are two performers.

In China, every year is represented by one of twelve animals.

According to legend, the ancient Chinese people scared away a terrible monster called Nian by decorating their homes with red lanterns and setting off noisy firecrackers.

Naadam

Naadam is a huge games festival. It began centuries ago as a way of training Mongolian armies and testing their skills. Every July, thousands of people get together to watch exciting wrestling matches, archery, and horse racing.

Contestants sing to their arrows to ask them to travel straight!

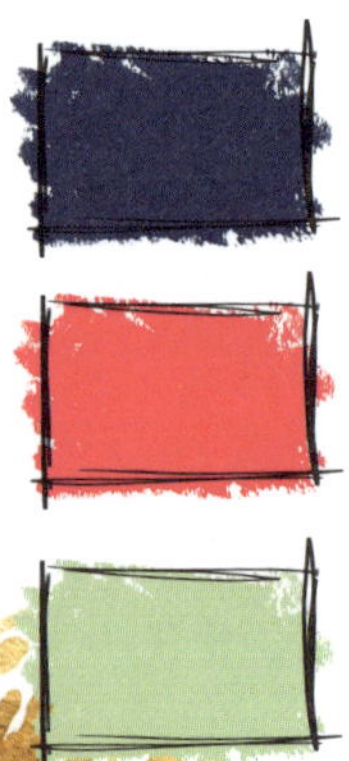

Try these colors.

Traditional arrows

Wrestling is the only game women aren't allowed to compete in.

Opening ceremony in the National Sports Stadium.

Up to 1,000 horses take part in the horse races, ridden by jockeys aged between five and 13 years old.

Pingxi Lantern Festival

The spectacular Taiwanese lantern festival is all about new beginnings, positive attitude, good luck, and goodwill. The breathtaking sight of thousands of glowing lanterns being released into the night sky is not to be missed!

Releasing a glowing lantern represents sending out wishes for a happy and successful new year.

Some lanterns are huge, like this amazing dragon!

Need to know:

An ancient legend says that once, the villagers of Pingxi fled their homes to hide from raiders. The lanterns were lit to let them know it was safe to return home.

Yeouido Cherry Blossom Festival

There are hundreds of cherry trees on the island.

For two weeks every spring, the island of Yeouido on the Han River in South Korea is filled with the stunning pink canopies of blooming cherry trees. Spring has arrived! People stroll through the scented streets and parks, enjoying parades, listening to musicians, and eating street food.

Cherry blossoms symbolize purity and beauty.

Some people dress up in traditional clothes to celebrate.

Cars are not allowed on some streets during the festival, so people can stroll around.

Marching bands play gongs and drums.

Songkran

p68

You're in for a soaking! Look out for the painted elephants.

Hungry Ghost Festival

p72

When ghosts come back to roam the earth.

Australia and Southeast Asia

Traditional ritual and ceremony meets high-spirited fun! The festivals in this region of big and small islands can be fun, solemn, or a little bit spooky . . .

Perfume Pagoda Festival

p70

Take a boat down the Yen River to ancient mountain temples.

New Year's Eve

p74

Start your year with a spectacular firework show.

Kai Festival

p76

Sample food cooked underground!

Songkran

Be prepared to get soaked! For three days every April, people crowd into the streets of Thailand to take part in the world's biggest water fight.

Hoses, buckets or water guns—anything goes!

Elephants spray the crowds with water from their trunks. They even get dressed up for the occasion!

Songkran is a Buddhist festival that marks the Buddhist New Year. People also visit Buddhist temples and take part in processions.

People pour water on statues of the Buddha to wash away the old year and make a good start for the new one.

Perfume Pagoda Festival

Lễ Hội Chùa Hương, or the Perfume Pagoda Festival, is the biggest festival in Vietnam. Every year thousands of people travel by road, then by river, then on foot or by cable car to the pagodas to pray for good health, wealth, and luck.

Need to know:

The Perfume Pagoda is a complex of Buddhist shrines and temples built into Huong Tich mountain, about 40 miles south of Hanoi.

Pilgrims travel from Hanoi (the capital of Vietnam), down the Yen River.

The first stop is usually the Den Trinh temple.

Dancers sometimes welcome pilgrims to the Thien Tru pagoda.

VIETNAM
The Thien Tru pagoda is over 500 years old!
VIETNAM · IMMIG
083A
07 SEP 20

Hungry Ghost Festival

Did you know that in Malaysia and countries across Asia, tradition says that the gates of the afterworld open for one month each year? People of Chinese descent living in countries all over Asia believe that during this time ghosts roam the earth, and celebrate the Hungry Ghost Festival to please these restless spirits.

Models of Tai Su Yeah, king of the land of the dead, watch over the wandering ghosts.

People burn fake banknotes and paper models of household objects for ghosts to use in the afterworld.

Try these colors.

Tua Pek Kong Taoist temple

In Taoist temples, prayers are said to help lost souls be reincarnated.

The ghosts are always hungry. Empty chairs are left at banquets so spirits can join the feast!

New Year's Eve

For a celebration you won't forget, join more than a million people celebrating at Sydney Harbour on New Year's Eve. At nine o'clock and midnight, the night sky explodes with the deafening bangs and glittering colors of eight tons of fireworks.

To get the best viewing spots, get there early!

Sydney Harbour Bridge is the largest steel arch bridge in the world.

The Opera House is covered in over a million self-cleaning tiles!

AUSTRALIA

About 100,000 fireworks illuminate the sky. The display costs around $5 million!

Kai Festival

New Zealand's population has a mix of people from Māori, European, and Pacific Islander descent. Māori Kai festivals celebrate Māori food. There's also lots of singing, dancing, chanting, and creativity.

Māori dancers "speak" to the spirits of their ancestors through moves and song.

Need to know:

In Māori hāngī cooking, stones are heated up, then put in a pit in the ground with food and covered up. After three hours, the food is cooked. Delicious!

Seafood (called kai moana) is another important part of Māori cuisine.

Māori art is created using wood, bone, stone, shells, flax, or tattooing, but the same flowing designs appear everywhere.

In the poi dance, dancers swing balls as they move.

Try these colors.

Your Festival

What's your favorite festival? Complete your journey to festivals around the world by creating a picture of a festival that happens in your own community!

Our coloring journey

Claire Sipi
(author)

I didn't realize there were so many fascinating festivals until I started my research. I just wanted to put down my pen and pack my suitcase!

Eva Byrne
(illustrator)

Creating the illustrations for this book was such a wonderful way to discover the exciting and interesting world we all share. Next stop, Dublin airport!

Kait and Craig Eaton
(designers)

Who knew there were so many amazing festivals and celebrations? Songkran looks like so much fun—we'd love to head to Thailand to experience it firsthand!

Photo credits Cover Elilarionova / Dreamstime.com and Laraclarence / dreamstime.com, 3 Thomasowen / dreamstime.com, 6 Kobby_dagan / dreamstime.com, 6 Vcarmstrong / dreamstime.com, 8 Ariel Skelley / Blend Images LLC / Getty Images, 8 Izanbar / dreamstime.com, 9 Mandritoiu / dreamstime.com, 9 Khabar / dreamstime.com, 10 Gjohnstonphoto / dreamstime.com, 10 Tatianatatiana / dreamstime.com, 11 Bdingman / dreamstime.com, 12 Beaustock / dreamstime.com, 13 Beaustock / dreamstime.com, 14 Puwanai / dreamstime.com, 15 Manamana / dreamstime.com, 15 Edenmanusphotography / dreamstime.com, 16 Imagecom / dreamstime.com, 17 Adpower99 / dreamstime.com, 18 Angelaostafichuk / dreamstime.com, 18 Byelikova / dreamstime.com, 18 Kobby_dagan / dreamstime.com, 19 Vcarmstrong / dreamstime.com, 20 Quasarphoto / dreamstime.com, 20 Donyanedomam / dreamstime.com, 21 Yurasova / dreamstime.com, 21 age fotostock / dreamstime.com, 23 Quasarphoto / dreamstime.com, 24 Yurasova / dreamstime.com, 24 age fotostock / dreamstime.com, 25 Mondan80 / dreamstime.com, 26 Deniskelly / dreamstime.com, 26 Donyanedomam / dreamstime.com, 27 Cicloco / dreamstime.com, 28 Kertuee / dreamstime.com, 29 Piccaya / dreamstime.com, 30 Ksenija2015 / dreamstime.com, 30 Sborisov / dreamstime.com, 31 Laraclarence / dreamstime.com, 31 Robin338 / dreamstime.com, 33 Bluiz60 / dreamstime.com, 33 SaigeYves / dreamstime.com, 34 Tsvirman / dreamstime.com, 34 Elilarionova / dreamstime.com, 35 Bogdan / dreamstime.com, 35 Scaliger / dreamstime.com, 36 Garlezki / dreamstime.com, 37 Sborisov / dreamstime.com, 37 Ksenija2015 / dreamstime.com, 38 Laraclarence / dreamstime.com, 39 Jakatics / dreamstime.com, 39 Laraclarence / dreamstime.com, 39 Joruba / dreamstime.com, 40 Tcon73 / dreamstime.com, 40 Robin338 / dreamstime.com, 41 Rasvanjp / dreamstime.com, 42 Homo Cosmicos / shutterstock.com, 43 Goldenkb / dreamstime.com, 43 Derejeb / dreamstime.com, 43 Chanelka005 / dreamstime.com, 44 Djembe / dreamstime.com, 44 Dietmar Temps / shutterstock.com, 45 Djembe / dreamstime.com, 46 Homo Cosmicos / shutterstock.com, 47 Homo Cosmicos / shutterstock.com, 48 Chanelka005 / dreamstime.com, 49 Goglik83 / dreamstime.com, 49 NORTHERN IMAGERY / shutterstock.com, 50 Goldenkb / dreamstime.com, 50 Belier / dreamstime.com, 52 Antonio Bugallo / Alamy Stock Photo, 53 Frizi / dreamstime.com, 53 Derejeb / dreamstime.com, 53 Fbxx71 / dreamstime.com, 54 Dipshelare / dreamstime.com, 55 unterwegs / shutterstock.com, 56 Sunilinpe / dreamstime.com, 56 Dipshelare / dreamstime.com, 57 Highviews / dreamstime.com, 58 Fishingner / dreamstime.com, 58 Thomasowen / dreamstime.com, 59 Izf / dreamstime.com, 60 Alexhor / dreamstime.com, 61 Pjworldtour / dreamstime.com, 61 Loca4motion / dreamstime.com, 62 unterwegs / shutterstock.com, 62 Wushoung / dreamstime.com, 64 Hanhanpeggy / dreamstime.com, 64 John_T / shutterstock.com, 65 Ake1150sb / dreamstime.com, 65 Chalamkhav / dreamstime.com, 66 Namfom Wittayakom / shutterstock.com, 67 Soheiladeli / dreamstime.com, 68 55146839 / dreamstime.com, 68 Hwannaa / dreamstime.com, 69 Yaryhee / dreamstime.com, 70 Cristatran / dreamstime.com, 70 Saaaaa / dreamstime.com, 71 Ngothyeaun / dreamstime.com, 72 Namfom Wittayakom / shutterstock.com, 72 Mr. Pops Photo / dreamstime.com, 73 Mosaic23 / dreamstime.com, 73 Sumnersgraphicsinc / dreamstime.com, 73 Xvaldes / dreamstime.com, 74 Soheiladeli / dreamstime.com, 75 Thecult / dreamstime.com, 75 Huating / dreamstime.com, 76 Brians101 / dreamstime.com, 80 Claire Sipi, 80 Eva Byrne, 80 Kait and Craig Eaton. All other images dreamstime.com and shutterstock.com.